# MONSTER JAM

# TRICKS, TRUCKS, AND STUNTS!

## An Insider's Guide to Monster Jam Marvels

# BY KIEL PHEGLEY

SCHOLASTIC INC.

# MONSTER JAM MAYHEM

From the growl of the massive engines to the roar of the packed crowds, everything in Monster Jam is bigger, bolder, and downright monstrous!

That's because Monster Jam is the only motorsport where trucks are transformed into crushing, acrobatic beasts. They speed through the pinpoint turns of a dirt racetrack! They crush the competition in freestyle rounds delivering one wow factor after another! They even defy gravity with wild jumps, tricks, and flips!

In this book, you'll learn how Monster Jam trucks power through venues around the globe. Meet each truck and discover its signature moves. Discover the next-level technology that powers these gigantic vehicles. Learn about the athletes behind the wheel who put the pedal to the metal.

Once you've read every page, you'll earn your place as the biggest Monster Jam fan ever!

# CONTENTS

# ALL ABOUT THE TRUCKS

From the rev of their engines to their spectacular finishes, the legend of Monster Jam is built on its competitor trucks. Inspired by epic creatures and driven with ruthless precision, each automotive beast is unique. And every Monster Jam truck tells a story with its most famous tricks, championship runs, and signature victories.

There is no better illustration of the Monster Jam style of competition than the intense rivalry between its two biggest icons: Grave Digger and Max-D.

For nearly 20 years, the Monster Jam World Finals was often a showdown between Grave Digger creator Dennis Anderson and Max-D originator Tom Meents. And in each face-off, one truck would reign victorious while one would get left in the dust.

So what makes these Monster Jam trucks so legendary? Read on to see how these rivals and more have made their mark!

# GRAVE DIGGER

ALL ABOUT THE TRUCKS

**O**ne of the most famous monster trucks in the world has been spooking out opponents for over 35 years! Grave Digger rolls into the Monster Jam arena with its glowing red eyes and graveyard body to bury any truck that gets in its way.

True to its name, Grave Digger was born from the automotive great beyond. In 1982, creator Dennis Anderson built the truck's original body out of an old 1957 Chevy Panel Wagon and discarded parts.

Digger's original red headlights came from old school buses! This Frankenstein-like creation may have earned laughs, but as Anderson promised, "I'll take this old junk and dig you a grave with it!" The truck soon drove any challengers . . . straight to the cemetery.

ALL ABOUT THE TRUCKS

Over the years of the Monster Jam tour, there have been 33 different models of Grave Digger wowing fans. Adding details like stronger suspension and spooky paint jobs, the truck has only gotten stronger. Today, a fleet of nine Diggers takes to the track across the world. That leads to the occasional "Digger vs. Digger" showdown in the annual Monster Jam World Finals. No matter how many models take to the dirt, only one Digger can win in the end. Talk about a bone-chilling race!

Thanks to its "need for speed" driving style, Grave Digger is one of the most decorated trucks in Monster Jam history. It's won five Racing World Championships—including in 2016 when it "Doubled Down" with both Racing and Freestyle trophies!

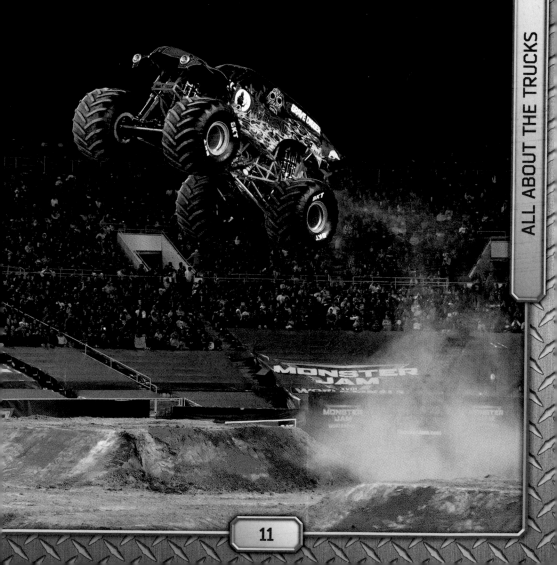

ALL ABOUT THE TRUCKS

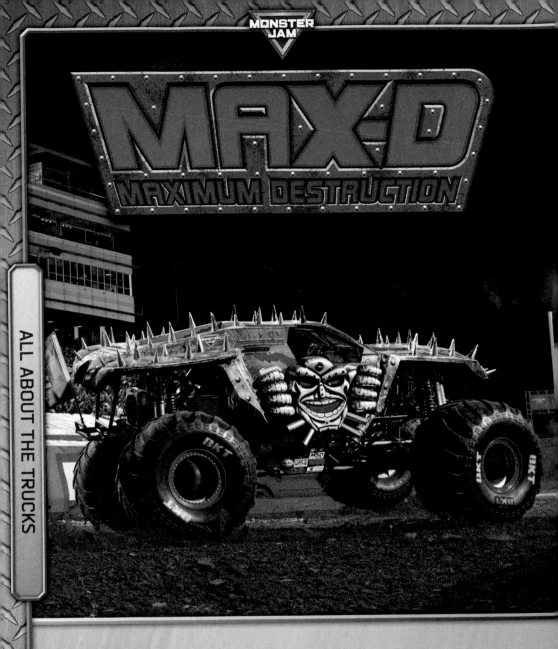

When you need to crank up the action as high as it can go, you call upon Max-D! That's the phrase that gives Monster Jam's most thrilling competitor its feared name. And it's a good thing the Monster Jam master called Max-D is covered in metal spikes. How else could it so easily shred the competition? Racking up more championship victories than any Monster Jam truck, Max-D represents taking it to the **MAX**.

To count this truck's victories, you'd need more than two hands. The armored futuristic SUV has taken home six overall racing championships and five freestyle honors at the World Finals. The biggest thrill in Monster Jam is watching Max-D take off in amazing freestyle feats.

That sound you hear is Max-D shattering expectations. One of the toughest Monster Jam trucks ever created, this metal-spiked monster makes an impact on every tour. The ultimate risk-taker, Max-D has never met a stunt it won't try until it meets perfection.

Backflips of all kinds. Wheelies that touch the sky. Dirt-spitting Donuts. Even car-crushing runs that flatten the track like a pancake! Max-D has done every major trick in the book and invented a few of its own along the way.

And from 2019 and beyond, Max-D opens up a new chapter in its storied history. This time, competitors feel the fury of Fire alongside its signature spikes . . .

## TOM MEENTS

For 15 years, Max-D's lead driver has been the Monster Jam super-star Tom Meents. Aside from being an 11-time World Champion, Meents has pioneered a number of tricks including the double backflip and the epic forward momentum backflip, making him Monster Jam's greatest daredevil.

# MONSTER JAM Fire & ICE

**M**onster Jam is a world where the hottest vehicles compete in the coolest competitions. And in the future of motorsports, fans will have to decide what side they're on: **Fire or Ice**.

On one side stands a lineup of Monster Jam trucks that represent fury and flame, steam and steel. These competitors hit the ground running hot and raise the temperature of every arena they run through. Get ready to feel the Fire or get burned!

Across the field roars the chilling, cunning, slick, and shocking Monster Jam trucks of Ice. Like an avalanche rumbling down from the snowiest mountain peaks, these are vehicles that will stop at nothing until they've frozen the field of play in their favor. They're cooler than cool. They're Ice cold!

Be on the lookout through this book for the stories of the trucks being transformed into Fire & Ice and then gear up for Monster Jam events where all six trucks clash in an elemental showdown.

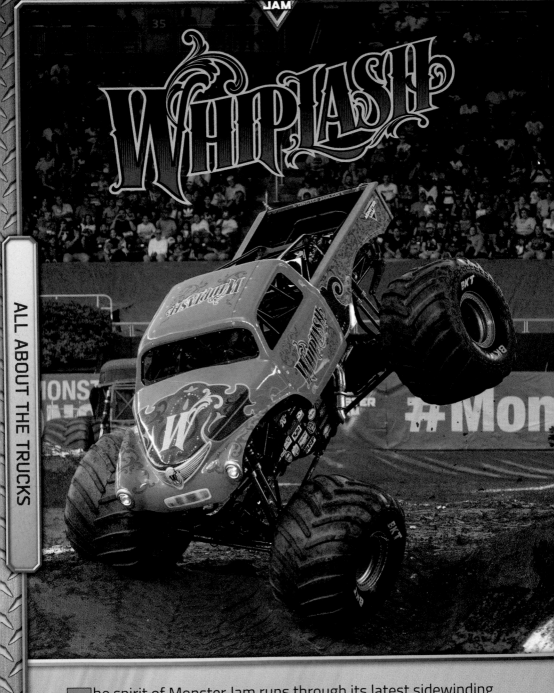

# WHIPLASH

The spirit of Monster Jam runs through its latest sidewinding competitor: Whiplash! This Western-themed truck can spin its dirt-slinging tires through any venue thanks to the sharp steering of fan-favorite driver, Brianna Mahon.

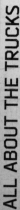

"Whiplash embraces the 'I don't ride, I drive' kind of lifestyle," Mahon explains. The inspiration for the truck was to make a Monster Jam competitor that was fierce and feminine without being drenched in pink. And Whiplash proves with each new competition that it's not just the boys who can get down and dirty in motorsports.

# BRODOZER

**M**onster Jam trucks don't settle for average, and the brawny beast called BroDozer takes engineering up a level. While most Monster Jam trucks run their engines on methanol, BroDozer is the first-ever diesel-powered vehicle in Monster Jam history. Thanks to the marvelous work of its design team, this titan burns mean . . . and clean.

The truck debuted in competition in 2018 with a rip-roaring freestyle run in Nashville. Shooting skyward with its engine revving up a whole new sound, BroDozer put the fans on their feet with a series of jumps sure to launch it into Monster Jam's upper ranks. BroDozer is driven by a new team of skilled drivers: Colt Stephens, and Heavy D and Diesel Dave from the *Diesel Brothers* TV show.

# DRAGONOID

he Dragonoid Monster Jam truck is inspired by one of the most incredible Bakugan ever discovered. This powerful new Monster Jam truck roars into every competition just like his namesake from Bakugan: Battle Planet. With ferocious molded detailing, Dragonoid takes to the skies with the most dynamic jumps and stunts. Truly reflecting the legendary Bakugan that inspired it, Dragonoid is a powerful beast on the track set to crush other trucks in any battle or competition. Staying true to the nature of all Bakugan, the Dragonoid truck is definitely ready to roll!

ALL ABOUT THE TRUCKS

# SCOOBY-DOO!

**R**uh-roh, Raggy! When you're at a Monster Jam show, get ready to scream for the mighty machine called Scooby-Doo. Inspired by the famous Hanna-Barbera cartoon canine, this Monster Jam truck avoids danger with a wacky and mischievous driving style fans can't get enough of.

Scooby has overcome its namesake's fears with some daring stunts and empowering feats. Scooby was the first truck with an all-women driving team.

# WONDER WOMAN

**D**C Comics' Amazon Warrior comes to life in the mighty Wonder Woman Monster Jam truck. The Wonder Woman Monster Jam Truck is known for its powerful moves and dynamic exterior. Keep an eye out for its extreme Donut spins, daring stunts, and extreme action as it crushes villainous cars in its way.

ALL ABOUT THE TRUCKS

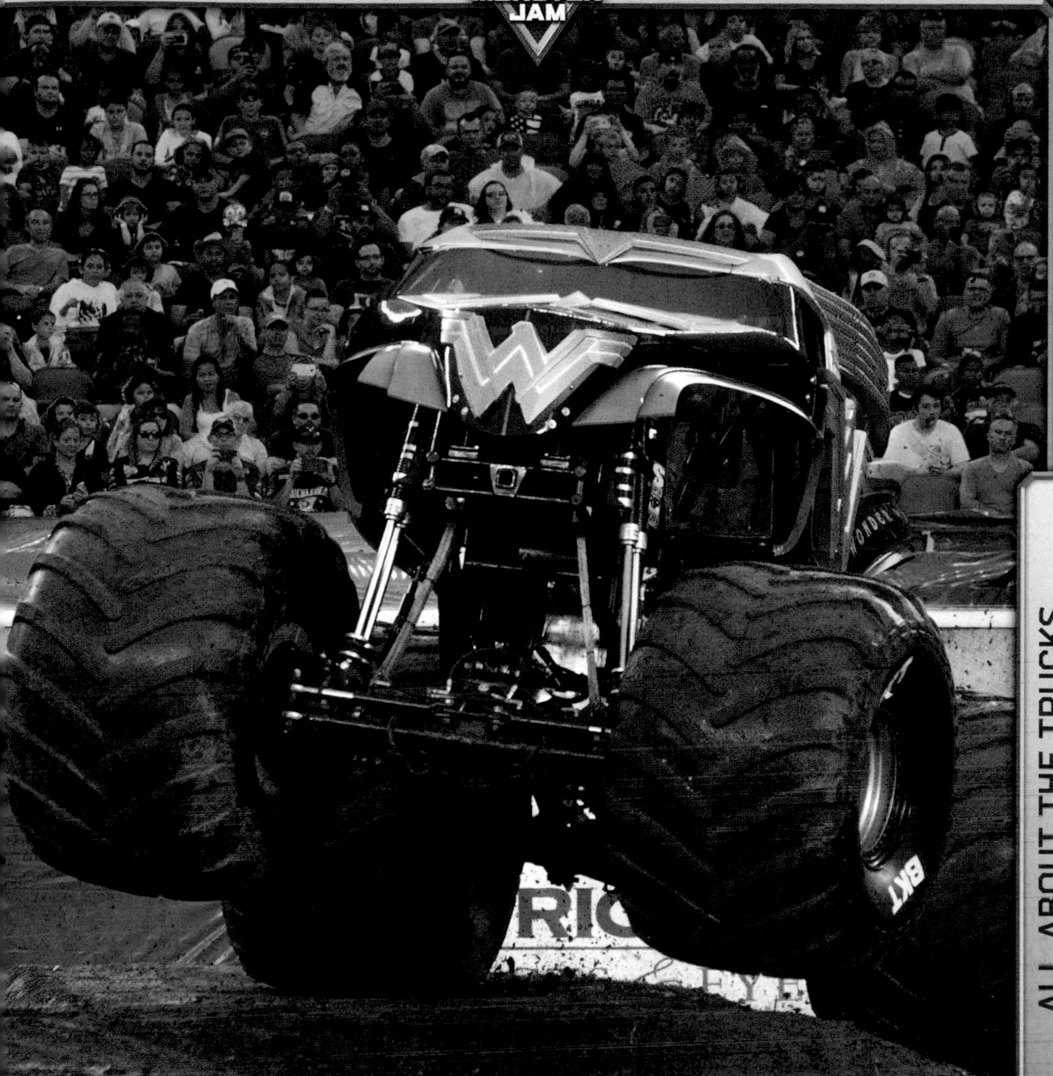
BKT

Ohio
BKT

Ohio

# RUFF AND TUFF: THE MONSTER MUTTS

## MONSTER MUTT®

ALL ABOUT THE TRUCKS

Other trucks better beware when the Monster Mutt pack is on the prowl. These tongue-wagging, teeth-chomping Monster Jam stars rock their 3D bodies with howling speed. From the original World Champion Monster Mutt, to the flashy Monster Mutt Dalmatian, right on through to the ruff Monster Mutt Rottweiler, there's a dog for everyone.

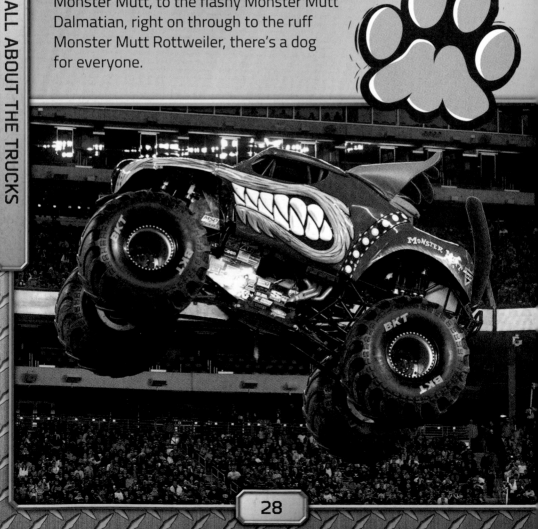

MONSTER JAM

# MONSTER MUTT
## DALMATIAN

# MONSTER MUTT
## ROTTWEILER

Just like a junkyard dog, the Monster Mutt team loves getting down and dirty in freestyle competitions. In fact, Monster Mutt won its only Freestyle World Championship in a tough 2010 competition by kicking up clouds of dirt as if it was digging for a bone.

Dalmatian got the crowd barking during a 2017 "Monster Jam® Triple Threat™" competition as a way to pump up the arena for additional Monster Jam ATV and Speedsters competitions following the truck's epic performance.

And in 2019, the spotted Mutt makes fans shiver with excitement when it wheels out its redesigned Ice look.

ALL ABOUT THE TRUCKS

# El Toro Loco ®

Like a beastly animal, the Monster Jam truck called El Toro Loco hits hard, horns and all. You don't need to wave a red cape to know that this bull runs flaming hot. One of the very first Monster Jam trucks to utilize a 3D "bolt on" shell, the crazy bull has steered and steamed its way into fans' hearts.

But El Toro Loco is more than its distinctive design. With its history of winning competitions and keeping a cool head, the truck has now become an anchor of the Ice squad in Monster Jam's Fire & Ice competitions.

**E**l Toro Loco is a freestyle superstar known for its wild and wicked runs full of wheelies, big jumps, and bigger crash landings. There's no obstacle this truck is afraid to charge! Each year, a slate of new faces teams with this classic bull to scratch a mark into Monster Jam history.

While a number of Monster Jam champions have gotten behind the wheel of El Toro Loco, none has a flashier style than Becky McDonough. When McDonough hits the track, she lets other drivers know that when she's on the field, a victory for El Toro is never far behind. But whether they see the smoke, the horns, or the flash of color first, competitors are always seeing red when El Toro Loco leaves them in the dust.

**Becky McDonough**

ALL ABOUT THE TRUCKS

MONSTER JAM

MEGALODON®

Like a denizen of the deep, Monster Jam's Megalodon can't stop moving toward its prey. Its radical shark-shaped shell makes it perfect for swimming through the dirt of the arena. Megalodon takes its name from a prehistoric shark whose name literally means "big tooth." This monster was the ancestor of today's Great White, and this truck strikes with the ferocity of both.

With its aerodynamic fins, Megalodon can pull off way more tricks than a fishtail. Only two years into its life as a Monster Jam truck, the shark turned heads at the 2018 World Finals with an unexpected top ten freestyle finish. The truck has also won the Monster Jam Triple Threat Series championship twice!

And the waters got warmer in 2019 when Megalodon joined Team Fire to burn up the record books as part of Monster Jam Fire & Ice.

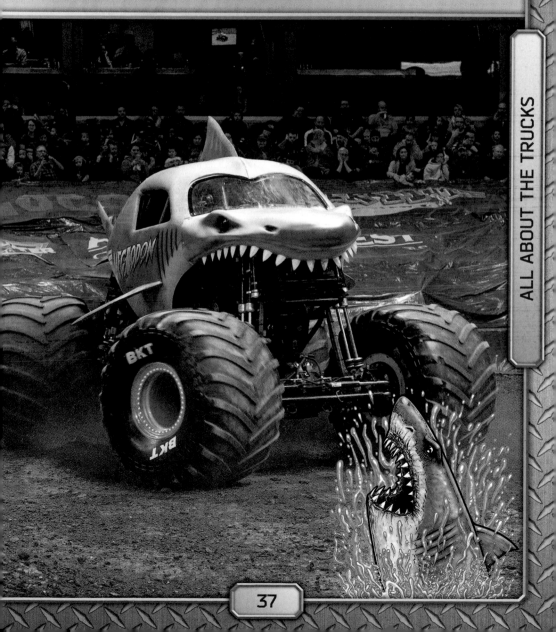

ALL ABOUT THE TRUCKS

**MONSTER JAM**

Dragon may be the Monster Jam truck based on a mythical creature, but its scaly skin makes its toughness all too real. With its 3D shell flaring out like the wings of its namesake, it's not uncommon to see Dragon take to the air. But with its cold, calculating part in Monster Jam's Fire & Ice series, all rules are off for how this monster will behave.

Dragon has proved its fury on the track! In 2016, the truck won the annual Double Down Showdown at the World Finals. As it roared in flame in the winner's circle, Dragon sent a message to the other trucks—if they cross it, they'll get burned.

# SON-UVA Digger ™

**W**ith a ripping racing record and an uncanny art style, Son-uva Digger definitely carries on the Grave Digger legacy. When iconic Digger creator Dennis Anderson announced his retirement, he had already introduced Monster Jam to a family legacy by welcoming three of his children into the league.

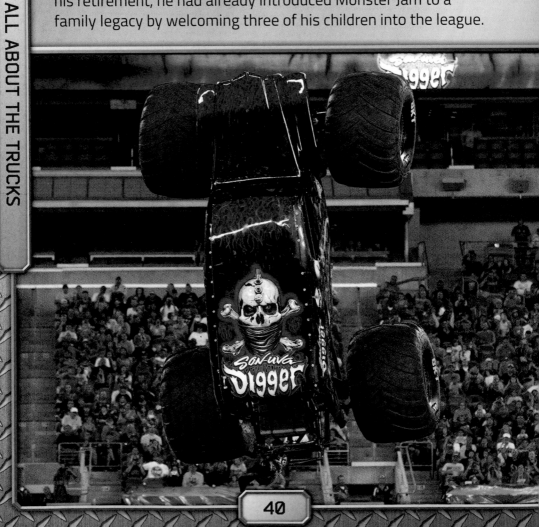

But with Son-uva, the continuation of the Grave Digger vibe has reached a new height. Dennis's son, driver Ryan Anderson, has kept up the family tradition of winning by delivering back-to-back championships in 2017 and 2018. Ryan describes his driving style as "out of control" and that is obvious to anyone in a Monster Jam stadium watching Son-uva race to victory!

ALL ABOUT THE TRUCKS

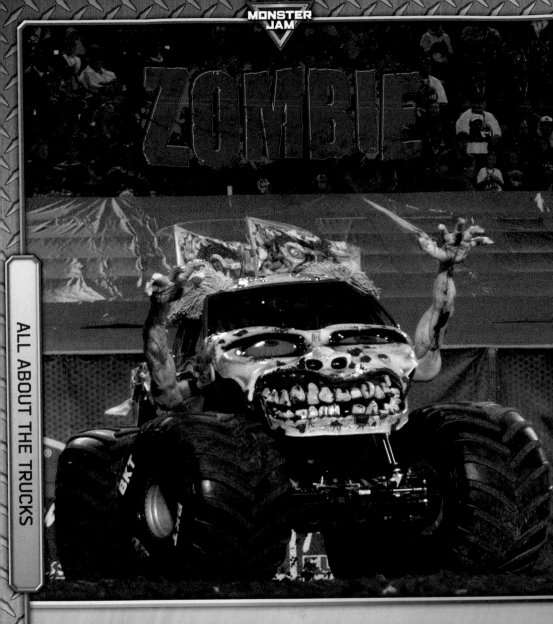

ZOMBIE

**W**ith its gruesome teeth and grabbing arms, Zombie is out to eat the competition alive. A World Finals fan favorite, this Monster Jam truck has a "stop at nothing" approach to freestyle, and its popularity is spreading through the crowds like a virus. Just watch the crowd as Zombie comes rolling through and fans throw up their Zombie arms in salute! Zombie will surely be raising temperatures as part of Monster Jam's Fire & Ice showdown.

Zombie is a ravenous competitor. This truck's driving style is anything but stiff as it's proven it can move faster than a film monster. The truck clawed its way toward a championship in the 2018 World Finals, narrowly losing out to Grave Digger. And since then, it's been hungry to win again.

# MONSTER JAM

# A L I E N
## INVASION

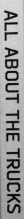
**S**oaring over Monster Jam like a thing from another world, Alien Invasion is the truck with otherworldly talents. Known for its lift-off jumps, this sleek competitor was last sighted beaming into the 2018 World Finals Double Down Showdown where it wowed the crowd with a spectacular crash landing. Is a full-scale Alien Invasion on the way? Look to the skies!

ALL ABOUT THE TRUCKS

# EarthShaker™

The rumbling you feel under your feet isn't an earthquake . . . it's EarthShaker! This Monster Jam truck combines the force of a seismic shift with the toughness of your favorite construction site dump truck. And in its few years in Monster Jam, EarthShaker has proven that crushing the dirt of the track is the best way to become a tour champion. Tristan England powered EarthShaker to a 2018 Triple Threat Series West championship.

On planet Earth, we measure the strength of a quake with the Richter Scale that runs from 0 to 9. But EarthShaker's power makes fans feel like they've been rocked all the way to 11. Of late, this truck has been spotted riding the fault lines across the ocean to impress Monster Jam fans in Europe. Here comes the big rift in the race!

S kimming the dirt track like a renegade boat on the high seas, Pirate's Curse casts a shadowy figure over Monster Jam. Rimmed with gold and armed against all enemies, this motor machine slashes its way through the arena with incredible speed. And you better believe that this Jolly Roger has more muscle than a simple skull and crossbones.

Frequent Curse driver Camden Murphy likes to get wild as he turns down the racing lanes and makes waves across the course. Like a pirate out for plunder, Camden Murphy is quite the multitasker! He's also a driving instructor and a NASCAR driver. It's no surprise Pirate's Curse has a thirst for victory. Yo-ho!

# SOLDIER FORTUNE™

MONSTER JAM

ALL ABOUT THE TRUCKS

Rigged with the strength and style of the military vets it honors, Soldier Fortune is Monster Jam's armed forces. With a hard camouflage shell that can meet the toughest terrain, its mission status is always set on victory.

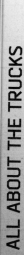

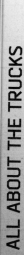

# MONSTER JAM

# SOLDIER FORTUNE
## BLACK OPS ™

ALL ABOUT THE TRUCKS

**D**aring and dangerous, the undercover Monster Jam truck called Soldier Fortune Black Ops glides through the arena with military confidence. Speaking of military confidence, Tony Ochs, the driver of Black Ops, is a veteran with real soldier experience. You might not see this truck coming until it's too late to beat.

MONSTER JAM

# Great Clips®
# MOHAWK WARRIOR

**F**rom the starting line to the top of a dirt ramp, fans are always looking up to Great Clips Mohawk Warrior. That's because the hair-raising look of this Monster Jam truck represents its jaw-dropping driving style on the track.

When the Great Clips Mohawk Warrior hits the venue, it keeps its jumps high and tight. Not content with the average style, the Warrior has been known to land consecutive backflips to keep fans head-banging their hair back and forth with excitement. Fans of all ages know wherever Great Clips Mohawk Warrior goes, It's Gonna Be Great!

# BLUE THUNDER

That sound you hear is Monster Jam's Blue Thunder rumbling into the arena, and like a storm, this truck always leaves the landscape changed. For over 15 years, Blue Thunder has shaken the competition with its powerful racing performances.

But just because Blue Thunder is one of the longest-running trucks on the Monster Jam circuit, that doesn't mean this storm-bringer can be blown out easily. The truck is an annual favorite of rookie drivers in the World Finals Double Down Showdown where in 2017 it tore through the racing competition so fast it blew out a tire.

# CHOOSE YOUR SIDE

**N**ow that you've met all the superstars of the Monster Jam tour, it's time to steel yourself for the Fire & Ice competition by choosing a side.

Burning up the ramps with fury are Team Fire. With Max-D on this side, you can bet that things will get hot enough to melt its raw metal spikes into an unstoppable hammer of a truck.

Meanwhile, Megalodon's Fire look will make your blood boil with pure excitement. And not to be outdone, Zombie is flush with brain-eating passion that will set your head ablaze.

For the fan that wants to slide into victory, there's the chilling stunts of Team Ice. With crystal horns pointed toward the ramps, El Toro Loco is shivering with energy. Monster Mutt Dalmatian bounds into the arena full of blue, blistering bluster. And Dragon has risen from its former life of flame to spew the cold breath of victory on anyone that stands in its way.

FIRE & ICE: CHOOSE YOUR SIDE

# ANATOMY OF A MONSTER

**M**onster Jam trucks are more than mechanical marvels. In order to be spotted from the highest heights of an arena, these rolling wonders must be works of art. That's why the body of every vehicle on the Monster Jam tour incorporates shocking paint jobs, monstrous "bolt-on" body parts, and colorful characters to stun fans at every turn.

ANATOMY OF A MONSTER

# The Graveyard

Deep in the heart of Kill Devil Hills, North Carolina, lies the Digger's Dungeon. This is the home base for all things **Grave Digger**, and it's where the world-famous Monster Jam truck revs up for competition. Every single fiberglass Grave Digger body is hand-painted at the Feld Entertainment headquarters in Palmetto, Florida, to let its eerie look strike fear into its competitors.

Like all Monster Jam trucks, Grave Digger is built on a reinforced steel chassis and then outfitted with a fiberglass shell. From there, not only are elements like the dual-steering mechanism and safety functions tested for perfection, engineers also add on elements like flags or Grave Digger's signature blaring red eyes.

The artists in Digger's Dungeon airbrush all of the **truck's** classic spooky scenes from its green and purple flames to its moonlit haunted house to the ghoulish mountaintop. But the most important aspect is the graveyard itself, where tombstones carry the names of trucks **Grave Digger** has buried in competition as well as members of its racing team. Freaky!

ANATOMY OF A MONSTER

Like its father, **Son-uva Digger** loves to deliver scares with its blue/purple design, but the story of this truck body is even more hardcore. Son-uva's design includes a jagged junkyard, where fallen competitors lay in broken piles. And eagle-eyed fans can spot the original versions of **Grave Digger** still lording over their bodies in the twilight.

# Detailed Designs

**M**onster Jam truck designs are some of the coolest in the world, and they help define the spirit of each vehicle in competition.

If you're more on the wild style, let **Whiplash** take you for a spin. Each element of this truck's Western-themed design was created to give **Whiplash** "tip-to-tail" details that demand to be viewed up close. The sharp final product will make you feel like you're riding the range as your head whips back and forth to watch it compete.

Thunder and lightning are a match made in the stormy sky, and **Blue Thunder** shows off its electrifying force with a lightning design. In its early days, the truck had the look of a darker rain cloud, but over the years, the energy of the competitor has been reflected with lightning that has spread across its body and strikes hard for victory.

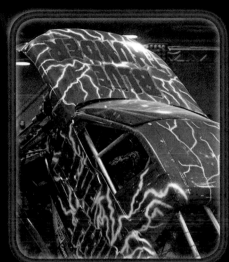

ANATOMY OF A MONSTER

Trucks don't come dirtier than construction vehicles, and **EarthShaker** lives up to that idea. When EarthShaker is done with a champion run, its blasting design of dirt makes it tough to tell where the track ends and the truck begins.

ANATOMY OF A MONSTER

or a truck not bound to this earth, **Dragonoid** fires up the detail from wingtip to tail spike. Like all the exciting monsters of *Bakugan: Battle Planet,* this truck is a splash of color with its crimson design heating up the track and revving up the hearts of Monster Jam fans everywhere.

ANATOMY OF A MONSTER

# Face-Off

**M**any Monster Jam trucks carry "bolt-on" elements that beef up their bodies beyond the average truck. But some of the most famous members of the tour literally face off with each other. These trucks put eyes, nose, teeth, and more right out front to build their unique personalities. They're more than Monster Jam trucks—they're machines with attitudes.

**Max-D**'s metallic alter ego is a robotic renegade that represents the truck's commitment to dismantling its foes. This twisted face rips its way out of the truck's body like an android out for adventure. Add in the truck's signature spikes, and nothing can stop this metal monster from tearing up the venue to the max.

Like the grim face of the Jolly Roger flag, **Pirate's Curse** chomps into the competition with its skull-based look. But its bolt-ons go beyond the face with its signature cutlass sword and swashbuckling hook hand. These added elements ensure the vehicle is a full-throttle scallywag ready to conquer.

# Hair-Raisers

The drivers may wear helmets, but making your hair stand on end is part of the job of a Monster Jam truck.

**Zombie** is a truck whose personality screams for one thing: braaaaains! But beyond its gruesome face, the vehicle's rigid arms, sagging skin, and hair complete the look that reaches into the hearts (and heads!) of the crowd. The look of Zombie's remaining hair patches may seem like follicles flattened by the grave, but that's just because they're made of cloth! The material keeps the truck untangled even if it rolls over in competition.

ANATOMY OF A MONSTER

Of course, no one piles their hair higher than **Great Clips Mohawk Warrior**. This truck's shocking spiked 'do never falls or folds during stunts. And the shock of purple that runs across its "scalp" gives the Warrior the kind of cool you just can't buy.

# The Dog Pound

**A**udiences howl whenever one of Monster Jam's canine competitors runs the track. That's because the likes of the **Monster Mutt** squad and **Scooby-Doo!** embody the best of man's best friend.

Each fiberglass body of Monster Jam's dog-based trucks starts with a mighty muzzle that pulls back to a ferocious set of teeth. But hounds are more than their bark or their bite, and so no mutt is complete without ears, tongues, and tails to make them come alive.

Last of all, each Monster Jam dog has a healthy coat . . . of paint that's specifically designed to mimic the fierce fur of their four-legged inspirations.

# Heroic Highlights

Some Monster Jam truck designs go past the monstrous and into the magnificent style of legendary heroes. **Wonder Woman** wows with its graceful style based on the world-famous superhero. But what really makes this truck a heroic tribute are the details in its body design.

When Monster Jam set down to replicate the superhero's costume, the goal was bringing out all of Wonder Woman's iconic gear alongside the essential truth of her awesomeness. That begins with the golden additions of her tiara and WW breastplate—each of which are as strong and stable as the hero's unbreakable Bracelets of Submission. But most important of all, the back of the truck features her evil-thwarting golden Lasso of Truth along for the ride.

ANATOMY OF A MONSTER

# Chrome Domes

To pump up the shine of the vehicles that are out of this world, Monster Jam adds stunning neon lights to both body and wheels. When **Alien Invasion** turns these on, they play off the pearly hand-painted body and Alien Invasion graphic for an out-of-this-world effect. As the monster mothership flies, the view is rarer and more radiant than a UFO.

ANATOMY OF A MONSTER

ANATOMY OF A MONSTER

The tough shells of Monster Jam's extraordinary vehicle competitors also carry the polished look of a decorated military uniform. That's because the dual competitors of the **Soldier Fortune** franchise come complete with streamlined style, whether it's a camouflage paint job or the most mysterious matte black finish of **Soldier Fortune Black Ops**.

# Mythic Monster Jam

**P**erhaps no truck designs better put the "Monster" in Monster Jam than the trio of beastly bodies on **El Toro Loco**, **Megalodon**, and **Dragon**. Whether in their classic modes or as part of the Fire & Ice competition, each of these fierce trucks has its own jaw-dropping features.

ANATOMY OF A MONSTER

Not only are its sharp horns always pointed towards victory, but El Toro Loco can snort real steam from its nose!

Megalodon is the perfect presentation of the ocean's greatest predator from its shark snout through to its fins and tail. These bolt-on elements are fabricated from foam to complete a unique 3D look across the whole truck body. This truck is fishing for trouble!

The most mythic of all Monster Jam trucks is more than a scaly exterior. Dragon doesn't just have a snarling look but a fire-breathing front to complete the legendary package. But that last effect is only used during special encore rounds when other vehicles in its way deserve more than a defeat . . . they need to be burnt to a crisp.

**ANATOMY OF A MONSTER**

# ALL ABOUT THE TRUCKS
## Team Max-D

When it comes to the many teams of drivers behind Monster Jam, it's no surprise that some of the highest-ranking athletes in the sport's history have been behind the wheel of Max-D.

Max-D's lead driver and creator is the legendary daredevil Tom Meents. The master of ridiculous flips and the roughest of freestyle skills for 25 years, this 11-time World Finals Champion describes his driving as "Chaotic, destructive, and for the Max-D fans."

Driving Max-D is a family affair for Meents's son Colton. He has created his own unique spin on Max-D's daring style with multiple championships to show for it.

Rounding out the team is Neil Elliott—a hard-working athlete on and off the Monster Jam field. Elliott earns his way into the World Finals year after year with daring freestyle runs, where he pulls out all the stops, rocketing wild tricks in Max-D until they're practically perfect.

Tom Meents

Colton Eichelberger

Neil Elliott

MONSTER TEAMS

# Team Grave Digger

MONSTER TEAMS

From the Graveyard to the winner's circle, the most celebrated Monster Jam truck is a family affair. That's because Grave Digger is a legacy vehicle that began with its creator and longtime driver, Dennis Anderson, who has since passed the truck on to his children after retirement.

Adam Anderson says of his stepping into the Digger suit, "It's always been my life. It's all I ever knew." And the athlete has proven how monumental the Grave Digger legacy is with five World Finals Championships in both racing and freestyle!

Krysten Anderson

Adam Anderson

Meanwhile, Krysten Anderson has impressed fans as the first full-time female driver of Grave Digger. "I'm an Anderson . . . you never know what you're going to see!" she teases.

And with so many trucks in competition, Team Grave Digger employs a virtual army of great athletes. Drivers like World Finals Racing Champion Morgan Kane, veteran wildman Charlie Pauken, Triple Threat Series champ Tyler Menninga, Brandon Vinson, and Randy Brown all add to the daring Grave Digger legendary troupe.

Tyler Menninga

# Team Scooby-Doo!

**R**unning other competitors out of the arena like ghosts out of a haunted amusement park is the signature of Scooby-Doo! And the athletes at the heart of Team Scooby-Doo! are a duo of ladies who are never afraid to defeat the baddies.

MONSTER TEAMS

Linsey Read

Myranda Cozad

MONSTER TEAMS

Linsey Read attacks the arena with the style of an off-road animal. And since joining Team Scooby-Doo!, this athlete has been squeezing as much adventure as possible into every run.

Myranda Cozad started as a diehard fan of Monster Jam, but she proved her racing talent on the ATV circuit before climbing into the Scooby-Doo! driver's seat. Cozad says her style "has become more and more aggressive. I love to get big air and keep the fans on the edge of their seats!"

# Team Monster Mutt

**J**ust like each hairy hound on the team has its own unique look, the drivers behind Team Monster Mutt own their epic styles without skimping on the vehicle's gritty growl.

MONSTER TEAMS

Cynthia Gauthier

Candice Jolly

Representing Monster Mutt Dalmatian are two drivers who are definitely on fire: Cynthia Gauthier and Candice Jolly. Gauthier calls herself "a certified adrenaline junkie" who uses her years as a motorcycle racer to rev up Dalmatian. Gauthier ices up the tracks as the driver for Monster Mutt Dalmatian Ice. Jolly is a more calculated driver with an eye for wicked tricks.

# Team El Toro Loco

**O**ne of the biggest trucks in Monster Jam history deserves one of the biggest teams, and El Toro Loco's athletes don't do anything small. They always take the bull by the horns!

MONSTER TEAMS

Kayla Blood

Mark List

For the speedsters in the crowd, watch for Kayla Blood, Chuck Werner, and Mark List. Blood promises that when she's on the track, she is "Aggressive and always giving it my all." Werner promises "I love anything with a motor that goes fast or goes big." List worked for years building tracks for Monster Jam, so he knows how to make the bull speed through the turns.

Becky McDonough

Armando Castro

But El Toro Loco has a wild freestyle side, too, and athletes Becky McDonough and Armando Castro both dig into that side. McDonough has mastered the art of the backflip. Castro has been crushing cars with El Toro from coast to coast. He is a former first responder and always knows how to keep it safe while pounding the pedals.

MONSTER TEAMS

# Team Zombie

**MONSTER TEAMS**

**T**eam Zombie attacks the competition of Monster Jam like roving hordes full of scares and shivers. Veteran driver Bari Musawwir admits that "Zombies creep me out," but that hasn't stopped him from having a sharp style that's equal parts planning and on-the-spot action. Similarly, Ami Houde delivers surprising technical feats even though Zombie may look like a creeper out of control.

Monster Jam fans across the globe know all about Alx Danielsson— the Swede with a need for speed. Representing Team Zombie on Monster Jam's European Tour, Danielsson brings his experience as a championship formula racer and stock car driver to Zombie and injects life into the global arena.

**Bari Musawwir**

**Ami Houde**

**Alx Danielsson**

# Team Megalodon

Alex Blackwell

**M**egalodon chomped its way to an Arena Freestyle of the Year award thanks to athlete Alex Blackwell, who is known for hot winning streaks.

Like the Megalodon shark his truck is named after, Justin Sipes is always on the hunt for perfection. Since joining Monster Jam, this fishing fanatic has been reeling in victories on tour, but no matter how deeply he bites into the league, he's never satisfied.

Justin Sipes

MONSTER TEAMS

# Whiplash

Brianna Mahon

**B**reaking new ground as the originating driver of Whiplash is fan-favorite athlete Brianna Mahon. This driver knows how to make all sorts of vehicles whip, spin, and flip as she explains, "I have been involved with motorsports for over 20 years. I raced motocross my whole life, then started racing professionally." It's no wonder Whiplash is already blowing fans away.

# Wonder Woman

**C**ollete Davis was ready to step into the role of Wonder Woman as soon as she arrived at Monster Jam, and just like the famed superhero, she's "aggressive and fun." With a fast-paced style honed through years of go kart racing, this athlete is a warrior on the track for Wonder Woman followers.

Collete Davis

**MONSTER TEAMS**

# Team BroDozer

**M**aking Monster Jam's first diesel truck a success requires a calculated approach both in the shop and on the track. Team BroDozer begins with creators Heavy D and Diesel Dave, who himself went through the wringer at Monster Jam University to up his trick-spinning skills.

On the road, BroDozer also welcomes the cunning driving skills of veteran Colt Stephens. Known for testing all his turns and tricks in the driver's seat before he even starts the engine, Stephens promises that the only way to make the truck a legend is through hard work and precise preparation.

# Team Alien Invasion

Look out for some of the coolest solo truck drivers on the Monster Jam tour. These dirt-slinging mavericks have worked to make their vehicles stand out from the pack.

Bernard Lyght

For an intergalactic show, look no further than the floating feats performed by Alien Invasion all across Monster Jam.

With Bernard Lyght at the wheel, Alien Invasion spins like a spaceship in total control. And this athlete began his Monster Jam career after a run performing in live superhero shows!

MONSTER TEAMS

# Monster Jam Mavericks

Ryan Anderson

MONSTER TEAMS

Ryan Anderson created Son-uva Digger as a tribute to his father's Grave Digger legacy, but the truck and driver have both written legends of their own with back-to-back championship performances in Racing and Freestyle in the 2017 and 2018 World Finals Championships.

In the skeleton ship that is Pirate's Curse, Camden Murphy uses a "smooth but aggressive" style to take other trucks completely by surprise.

Camden Murphy

Second-generation Monster Jam driver Tristan England loves to keep fans on the edge of their seats from the top of EarthShaker when it hits the arena hard and fast.

**Tristan England**

**Bryce Kenny**

MONSTER TEAMS

The driver set to raise the buzz on Great Clips Mohawk Warrior is Bryce Kenny. With a background in dragster racing and a style he calls "tenacious," no one is better prepared to shave off a few seconds while racing the Warrior.

# FACE-TO-FACE

Sometimes competition for Monster Jam supremacy goes beyond the name on the side of your truck. And for the six competitors dominating Monster Jam's Fire & Ice era of competition, the driving factor in their season will be either the ability to remain cool under pressure or set the venue ablaze.

Team Ice looks to freeze out all competition with a trio of drivers known for their slick style. Revving up El Toro Loco Ice is **Scott Buetow**, a competitor who's never missed a World Finals since he joined the league over a decade ago. Barking up alongside the cool blue Toro is **Cynthia Gauthier** in Monster Mutt Dalmatian Ice. Already a fan favorite in the spotted canine crusher, Gauthier is ready to show what she can do with a little ice in her veins. And not to be outdone, **Jon Zimmer** is flipping the myth on its finned head by driving Dragon Ice. An enthusiastic snow boarder, Zimmer has what it takes to drive this blue beast into the winner's circle.

Torching up the track is Team Fire with three athletes who know how to perform when things get hot. No one else could control the explosive might of Max-D Fire than its creator **Tom Meents**. On tour there's no doubt he'll jump the truck through walls of sparks, flames, and the roar of the fans. With blazing speed, Zombie Fire's **Paul Strong** is looking to prove that a young driver can light the fuse of victory. And raising the temperature of the venue like a boiling ocean is all in a day's work for Megalodon Fire's **Cory Rummell**, who wows with an unexpected, trick-laden style.

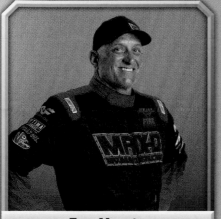

Tom Meents

Cynthia Gauthier

Cory Rummell

Jon Zimmer

Paul Strong

Scott Buetow

FIRE & ICE: FACE-TO-FACE

# MONSTER JAM AUTOGRAPHS

**W**hen you get the chance to meet the superstar athletes of Monster Jam, be sure to ask for an autograph, snap a picture and get all your questions answered about what it takes to be a great driver!

**Monster Jam Driver**

**Monster Jam Driver**

**Monster Jam Driver**

Before any Monster Jam tour stop, fans have a chance to attend the Pit Party. Anyone can pose for a picture in front of their favorite trucks on display. And you can attend meet and greets with your favorite drivers! The Pit Parties are an extra fun way to liven up a day spent at the Monster Jam Show.

**Monster Jam Driver**

**Monster Jam Driver**

**Monster Jam Driver**

 MONSTER JAM AUTOGRAPHS

MONSTER JAM AUTOGRAPHS

**Monster Jam Driver**

**Monster Jam Driver**

**Monster Jam Driver**

**Monster Jam Driver**

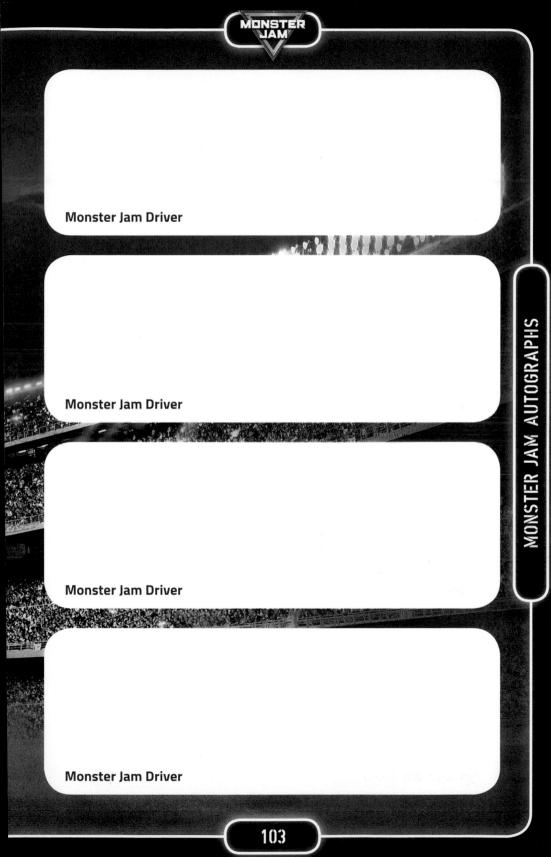

**Monster Jam Driver**

**Monster Jam Driver**

**Monster Jam Driver**

**Monster Jam Driver**

# MONSTER MACHINERY

**N**ow that you know what makes each Monster Jam truck fearsome and furious, it's time to learn about how the athletes behind the wheel speed for success. And that starts with the super-tough, ultra-safe Monster Jam suit.

## Suit Up

Every driver protects their head with a helmet that includes a fire-resistant face shield. Combine this with the **Head and Neck Support** (or **HANS**) harness, and everything from the neck up is ready for the roughest ride.

Not only is the Monster Jam suit styled to match the design of the driver's truck, it's also a three-layered fire suit that no flames can penetrate.

To top it all off, Monster Jam drivers wear specially designed gloves and shoes that keep them in control. Their grips are just tacky enough to stick to the steering wheel, while the shoes have a tough but thin bottom perfect for pushing down the pedals.

# EPIC ENGINEERING

**W**hat makes a Monster Jam truck go so fast? It's the insane engineering underneath the body that drivers can push to the max! Crowds go wild for the nonstop action at every Monster Jam tour, and without the incredible power of the innovative machinery, the show would hit the brakes.

This mechanical might starts with the truck engines—a special style of motor that runs on methanol. These engines sit in the middle of the chassis for optimal balance and can rev up to over 1,500 horsepower. That kind of force on a normal car would make the vehicle go over 260 miles per hour. But in a beastly Monster Jam truck, that motor can move a competitor over 60 miles an hour. That's speedy for a huge vehicle. Whoa, Nellie!

All told, the weight of a Monster Jam truck from motor to body is 12,000 lbs . . . only 1,000 lbs lighter than an African elephant! That's why drivers need to run up ramps at top speeds in order to pull off gravity-defying jumps and flips.

Everything else a Monster Jam truck does relies on the strength of its signature BKT tires. These massive tires measure 66 inches tall. That's one inch higher than the height of the average American! Tires on average cars are usually only a foot tall and weigh 20 pounds. Monster Jam truck tires weigh 645 pounds!

But these tires are so much more than a tall ride. They're pumped with more air than the average tire to make sure they can be a cushion for massive Monster Jam jumps. Yet, they actually only contain 24 PSI in tire pressure. A lot less than you would guess! The outside of each tire is custom made by BKT for Monster Jam.

When a Monster Jam truck comes gliding off a ramp or rolling over an arena obstacle, it can bounce, balance, or spray dirt for outstanding stunts!

MONSTER MACHINERY

The other major component of a Monster Jam truck's machinery is the system of shocks that connect the wheels and the axles of the truck. These super-tight coils use nitrogen to pack in hydraulic fluid and give the vehicles some outstanding springs.

The shocks allow a truck to land on the track without bursting the tires or breaking the body. In fact, these shocks are so absorbent of force that they allow a Monster Jam truck to jump as high as 30 feet without breaking anything. That's as high as jumping over two full-grown giraffes stacked on top of each other!

Of course, no truck would be complete without a steering wheel. And Monster Jam athletes are able to control how their vehicle moves in more ways than one.

The traditional steering wheel that sits high in the truck's seat only controls the front two wheels. This allows the driver to turn the vehicle left or right. But when it comes to spinning a major trick or hitting a jump full-bore, athletes must use a special rear-steering toggle switch that controls how the back tires turn.

Monster Jam drivers are so good at this dual-steering system that they pull pinpoint turns like they have "eyes in the back of their heads."

Safety is always a chief concern for Monster Jam. No matter how wild a ride gets, the driver always walks away from a big rollover or crash in terrific shape.

At every Monster Jam show, officials stand by with their finger on a radio device called the Remote Ignition Interrupter. That means they can cut the power to a truck's engine at any point, and the athlete just has to stick along for the ride.

Drivers are strapped into their custom-molded seats with a five-point safety harness that holds them in place even if their truck's body is crunching and crashing after a major trick.

# TRICKED OUT

**W**hether they're zipping through the turns of a neck-and-neck race or busting their way across the ramps of a freestyle arena, Monster Jam trucks are best known for their amazing tricks and stunts. These are the kinds of unstoppable motorsport acts you can only get from Monster Jam!

## Speed Demons

**H**ow fast can Monster Jam trucks go? Well, let's just say you should never leave your seat. Even with their massive size, these vehicles are capable of driving over 60 miles per hour in a live event. Monster Jam trucks are known to rip through an entire obstacle course in less than 16 seconds!

TRICKED OUT

# Two-Wheel Skills

The most iconic trick in a Monster Jam driver's freestyle arsenal is the Wheelie, but these trucks have gone far beyond popping up a front tire like you do on your bike. Sometimes, they bounce into the move by slamming their tires off the track in what is called a **Slap Wheelie**.

TRICKED OUT

Aside from the classic move that lifts a truck up on its back tires, Monster Jam competitors are known for **Stoppies**, where they tilt up on their front tires and drive with their tailgates high in the air.

TRICKED OUT

Speaking of air, look out for when a
Monster Jam truck launches up a ramp and into a
**Sky Wheelie**. With this signature move, the vehicle lifts off
the ground in a vertical jump that's cooler than a rocket launch.

# Tire Terrors

**W**ith bounce and bite beyond anything in motorsport, the spinning circles that are Monster Jam's massive tires accomplish more tricks than you can sling a hubcap at.

When in a tight spot, the best athletes know to switch up their vehicle by pulling off a **Bicycle**. This trick involves riding up on any two wheels along the same side of the truck and zipping along just like a BMX bandit.

To get ahead, sometimes you've got to go backwards. That's what the **Reverse Popper** is for—a move that sees a truck set its back tires on a ramp with a quick injection of reverse power. The truck propels the front tires off the ground and into the record books.

Sliding back sometimes takes on a style all its own with the dance-inspired **Moonwalk**. That's when an already awe-inspiring Stoppie starts to move as the vertically inclined truck drives backwards with effortless ease.

**TRICKED OUT**

# Donut Dangers

For fans who like their tricks down and dirty, there's nothing better than the classic dirt-throwing **Donut**. With its nose pointed in and its rear tires spinning around, a Monster Jam truck practically drills a hole in the dirt in the shape of the classic glazed treat.

When two tires come off the ground during a Donut and the driver keeps on driving, they're hitting a **Cyclone Donut**. Trucks can fly right off the ground if they get going fast enough. Tires hitting the air are something you don't want to miss at a Monster Jam show!

# Flipping Out

Seeing is believing when it comes to the one-of-a-kind stunt that is a Monster Jam truck **Backflip**. This daring drive can only be completed by running at a vertical ramp full-throttle and letting the force toss itself up in the air and back again. In short: it's not for the faint of heart!

Monster Jam drivers have taken to upping their game in recent years, creating the special **Corkscrew Flip** that lets the truck spin side-to-side in midair like an aerial Donut!

TRICKED OUT

Most impressive of all is the almost impossible **Forward Flip**. Driver Tom Meents had to build a special ramp and practice for years in order to send Max-D headfirst into the history books, but it was well worth the wait.

# Big Air Bonanza

The big finale of any Monster Jam show is the moment when the trucks go for their most epic **Big Air Jumps**. Aside from popping up 30 feet or more in the air, these trucks can also launch forward for over 130 feet.

In 2016, driver Tom Meents performed one of the wildest **Long Jumps** in Monster Jam history. He jumped his vehicle over six other Monster Jam trucks without touching one. That's like jumping over more than 18 cars in one fell swoop!

# EXPERIENCE THE FURY OF
# MONSTER JAM

SEE MONSTER JAM LIVE! CHECK OUT A TOUR NEAR YOU AT ANY OF THE PERFORMANCES ACROSS FIVE CONTINENTS.